MAUI

TRAVEL GUIDE 2024-2025

Your Essential Companion to Exploring the Island's Pristine Beaches, Hidden Gems, and the Spirit of Aloha.

Cedric J. Stone

COPYRIGHT

TABLE OF CONTENTS

Gratitude

Dear Readers,

Thank you for choosing this book to guide you on your next adventure. Your interest and curiosity are greatly appreciated, and I am grateful for the chance to share the beauties of our world with you. Before you begin the adventures detailed within these pages, I'd like to express my heartfelt gratitude.

Your support means everything to me, and I am confident that this book will be a valuable companion on your journey. Whether you're planning your first vacation or returning to uncover new treasures, you'll find inspiration, practical insights, and a greater bond with the places you visit.

Enjoy every second of your journey, and may your memories be as breathtaking as the sights you will see.

Thank you for your participation in our adventure.

MAUI, HAWAII MAP

SCAN ME

HOW TO SCAN THE QR CODE

1. Open your smartphone's camera or QR code scanner app.
2. Point the camera at the QR code.
3. Wait for the camera to recognize the code.
4. Tap the notification or link that appears.
5. Follow the link or instructions provided.

INTRODUCTION

Welcome to Maui

Maui, also known as "The Valley Isle," is a jewel in the Hawaiian peninsula, embodying the spirit of aloha and offering a diversified tapestry of natural beauty, rich culture, and dynamic activities. Maui, Hawaii's second-largest island, is known for its breathtaking scenery, which includes lush jungles and towering volcanoes, as well as beautiful beaches and bright coral reefs. This introduction delves into what makes Maui a must-see destination, emphasizing its unique history, culture, and the diverse experiences available to visitors.

The Allure of Maui

Maui's allure stems from its remarkable diversity. The island is 727 square miles and has a population of around 165,000 people, making it a welcome and intimate location for travelers. The island's terrain is characterized by two major volcanic peaks: Haleakalā, which reaches over 10,000 feet above sea level, and the West Maui Mountains, which provide magnificent views and possibilities for adventure.

Maui's beaches are legendary, spanning over 30 miles of pristine shoreline and ranging from white to black and red sand beaches. Maui's natural beauty offers amazing experiences, including relaxing on the shores of Kaanapali Beach, snorkeling in the crystal-clear waters of Molokini Crater, and viewing the sunrise at Haleakalā National Park.

A Brief History of Maui

Maui's history is as fascinating as its landscapes. The island was formed by volcanic action millions of years ago, and its earliest inhabitants are believed to have come from Polynesia around 1,500 years ago. These early inhabitants established a prosperous culture based on agriculture, fishing, and community life known as the ahupua'a system, which divided land into sustainable pieces from mountain to sea.

In the late 18th century, European explorers, particularly Captain James Cook, established contact with the Hawaiian Islands, causing profound changes in the islands' social and economic structures. Maui was essential to the unification of Hawaii under King Kamehameha I, who led a victorious campaign from the island to capture the adjacent islands.

Christian missionaries arrived in the nineteenth century, bringing with them new religions, educational systems, and agricultural practices. The sugarcane industry thrived, attracting immigrants from China, Japan, Portugal, and the Philippines, adding to the multicultural tapestry that distinguishes Maui today.

Why Visit Maui in 2024-2025?

Maui, Hawaii, remains a top destination for travelers seeking unparalleled natural beauty, adventure, and relaxation. In 2024-2025, Maui offers even more reasons to visit. With its pristine beaches, lush rainforests, and vibrant local culture, the island promises a unique blend of experiences.

One of the standout attractions is the newly renovated Haleakalā National Park, where you can witness breathtaking sunrises above the clouds and explore scenic hiking trails. Whale watching in the winter months is at its peak, as humpback whales migrate to the warm Maui waters—an awe-inspiring sight that attracts visitors from around the world.

Maui's culinary scene is also thriving, with an emphasis on farm-to-table dining and sustainable practices. Fresh seafood, locally grown fruits, and traditional Hawaiian dishes make for unforgettable dining experiences. For those seeking adventure, Maui's diverse landscape offers opportunities for snorkeling at Molokini Crater, exploring the lush Hana Highway, or surfing the legendary waves of Ho'okipa Beach.

The island's commitment to sustainability and eco-tourism is also more evident than ever, with numerous initiatives aimed at preserving its natural beauty. This aligns perfectly with the growing trend of responsible travel.

Whether you're drawn by the allure of its stunning landscapes, the thrill of outdoor activities, or the charm of its small towns and vibrant culture, Maui in 2024-2025 offers something for every traveler. With its warm aloha spirit and endless opportunities for exploration, it's no wonder Maui remains a must-visit destination.

How to Use This Guide

Welcome to your essential Maui travel guide! This resource is designed to help you navigate the island with ease, offering insider tips, must-see attractions, and practical advice to make your trip unforgettable.

Start by exploring the "Top Attractions section", which highlights the island's most iconic spots—from the breathtaking Road to Hana to the stunning beaches of Wailea. Each entry includes essential information, such as the best times to visit, fees, and unique experiences you shouldn't miss.

Next, dive into the "Activities and Adventures" chapter, where you'll find recommendations for outdoor enthusiasts, from snorkeling and surfing to hiking and ziplining. Whether you're an adrenaline junkie or prefer leisurely walks along the beach, there's something for everyone.

For food lovers, the "Dining and Cuisine" section guides you through Maui's culinary scene, featuring everything from local food trucks to fine dining. Discover where to find the best poke, shave ice, and farm-to-table delights.

Our "Accommodations" section helps you choose the perfect place to stay, whether you're looking for luxury resorts, Mid-range hotels and inns, or budget-friendly options. We've also included practical tips on transportation, packing, and safety to ensure a smooth and enjoyable trip.

Use this guide to plan your itinerary, navigate the island, and uncover hidden gems. Whether you're visiting for the first time or a seasoned traveler, this guide is your companion for an unforgettable Maui adventure. Enjoy your journey—aloha!

CHAPTER ONE

Practical Information

When planning a trip to Maui, having practical information at your fingertips is critical to ensuring a seamless and pleasurable visit. This chapter provides comprehensive insights into the vital aspects of travel planning, such as climate, visa regulations, currency, language, health and safety tips, and much more. Whether you are a first-time visitor or a seasoned tourist, this guide will equip you with the knowledge you need to make the most of your visit to this enchanting island.

Climate and Best Time to Visit

Maui's climate is as diverse as its scenery, with year-round mild temperatures ranging from the mid-70s to mid-80s Fahrenheit (24 to 30 degrees Celsius). The island has two main seasons: the dry season (kau) from April to October, and the wet season (hooilo) from November to March. Here is a closer look at the two seasons:

Dry Season (April to October):
This is the most popular period to visit Maui, with mild temperatures and low humidity levels. The island is teeming with activity, and all of the attractions are open. It's the perfect season for outdoor activities like hiking, swimming, and touring the Road to Hana.

Wet Season (November to March):
During this period, Maui experiences more rainfall, especially in the lush, tropical areas of the island. However, the rain is usually short-lived, and there are still many sunny days. Humpback whales migrate to Maui's waters from December to April, making this the ideal time to see them.

Each season has its own distinct appeal, so the best time to visit depends on your interests and tastes. Be sure to book accommodations and activities in advance, especially during busy travel periods.

Visa and Entry Requirements

For most visitors, visiting Maui is straightforward, but it's important to be informed of entry requirements before you arrive.

- **United States Citizens:** U.S. citizens do not need a visa to travel to Maui, as Hawaii is a state within the United States. A valid government-issued ID, such as a driver's license or passport, is required for air travel

- **International Visitors**: Visitors from nations participating in the Visa Waiver Program (VWP) can travel to the United States for tourism or business for up to 90 days without a visa. Prior to boarding their flight, individuals must have an approved Electronic System for Travel Authorization (ESTA). Travelers from other countries must apply for a tourist visa (B-2) at a United States embassy or consulate.

Before planning your trip, make sure to check the US Department of State website for the latest information on visa requirements and travel advisories

Currency and Exchange Rates

Maui's official currency, like the rest of the United States, is the US dollar (USD). Here are some recommendations for managing your finances while you're staying:

- **Currency Exchange:** Currency exchange services are provided at Kahului Airport, major banks, and certain hotels. However, exchange rates may be less favorable than those provided by banks or ATMs.

- **ATMs and Credit Cards**: ATMs are widely distributed throughout the island, and most businesses take major credit cards such as Visa, MasterCard, and American Express. It's a good idea to notify your bank about your travel intentions to avoid problems with card transactions.

- **Tipping:** Tipping is customary in Maui and is typically required in restaurants, bars, and for services such as taxis and tour guides. The standard tip is between 15-20% of the whole bill.

Language and Useful Hawaiian Phrases

English is the primary language spoken in Maui, making communication simple for most travelers. However, incorporating a few Hawaiian terms and phrases into your conversations can improve your overall experience and demonstrate respect for the local culture. Here are a few useful phrases;

- **Aloha:** Hello, goodbye, or love.
- **Mahalo:** Thank you.
- **Ohana.** Family.
- **Kokua:** Help or Assistance.

- **E komo mai:** Welcome.

Using these phrases can help you communicate with locals and show your admiration for Maui's culture.

Health and Safety Tips

Maintaining your health and safety when traveling is a primary priority. Here are some vital suggestions for being safe and healthy on your trip to Maui:

- **Health Care:** Maui has several healthcare facilities, including hospitals, urgent care clinics, and pharmacies. It is recommended to get travel insurance that covers medical situations, as healthcare in the United States can be expensive.

- **Sun Protection:** Because Maui's tropical climate provides plenty of sunshine, protecting yourself from harmful UV rays is critical. Wear high-SPF sunscreen, a wide-brimmed hat, and sunglasses, and seek shade during the warmest hours of the day.

- **Ocean Safety:** The ocean is one of Maui's biggest attractions, but it can also be unpredictable. Always swim at lifeguarded beaches, follow warning signs, and be wary of strong currents and waves.

- **Wildlife Awareness:** While Maui is typically safe, visitors should appreciate the island's animals. Keep a safe distance from creatures like sea turtles and monk seals, and don't feed or touch them.

- **Hydration and Nutrition:** Staying hydrated is critical, especially when engaging in outdoor activities. Carry a reusable water bottle and take advantage of the island's fresh fruits and local food to maintain a healthy diet.

Transportation

Navigating Maui is reasonably simple, with many transit alternatives to suit varied preferences and budgets. Here are the available transportation options in Maui:

- **Car Rentals:** Renting a car is the most convenient method to see Maui, allowing you to reach isolated areas and travel at your leisure. Rental firms are located at Kahului Airport and in major towns.

- **Public Transportation:** Maui Bus provides economical public transportation with routes that serve popular areas. While it is a less expensive choice, some of the more outlying attractions are inaccessible.

- **Taxis and Ride-Sharing:** Taxis and ride-sharing services such as Uber and Lyft are available, however they are more expensive than other options. They're ideal for short journeys and airport transfers.

- **Biking and Walking:** Biking is a popular way to explore specific locations, particularly the towns of Lahaina and Paia. Walking is ideal for discovering smaller towns and beachside locations.

Communication and Ensuring Connectivity

Staying connected on your trip to Maui is easy, with various alternatives for telephone and internet access. Here are the available communication outlets in Maui:

- **Mobile Phones:** Most major US carriers provide coverage in Maui, but if you're visiting from outside, you should check with your provider about roaming charges. If you expect to use your phone frequently, consider acquiring a local SIM card.

- **Internet Access:** Wi-Fi is readily available in hotels, cafes, and public spaces. Some motels may charge for Wi-Fi access, so verify ahead of time.

- **Emergency Contacts:** In the event of an emergency, call 911 for urgent assistance. Keep a list of crucial contacts, such as your hotel and travel insurance provider, ready.

Sustainable Travel Practices

Maui's natural beauty is a gift that should be protected for future generations. Practicing sustainable travel can help conserve the environment while also supporting the local community. The following are core elements to practicing sustainable travel:

- **Respect Nature:** Follow defined routes, avoid picking plants or flowers, and properly dispose of rubbish. Participate in beach cleanups or volunteer activities to help the community.

- **Support Local Businesses:** To help the local economy, choose locally owned restaurants, shops, and tour operators. Buy locally manufactured products and crafts as mementos.

- **Reduce Plastic;** Carry a reusable water bottle, bags, and utensils to reduce plastic waste. Many Maui businesses are attempting to minimize single-use plastics, and you can join them.

You are now equipped with practical knowledge and ready to embark on a memorable journey to Maui. Whether you're exploring its breathtaking scenery, immersing yourself in its rich culture, or simply relaxing on its magnificent beaches, Maui provides a one-of-a-kind experience that will leave an indelible imprint. Accept the spirit of aloha and revel in the magic of this wonderful island.

CHAPTER TWO

Getting to Maui

Maui, the second-largest island in the Hawaiian peninsula, is a haven for travelers seeking sun, sand, and adventure. Maui is well-known for its diverse landscapes, which include volcanic craters, lush jungles, and clean beaches. This chapter provides a comprehensive guide to getting to Maui, covering everything from vacation planning and flight booking to navigating the island's transportation options once there.

Planning Your Trip To Maui

Choosing The Right Time To Visit

When planning a trip to Maui, scheduling is extremely important. While the island is a year-round destination, understanding the seasons and their impact will help you get the most out of your vacation. Here's what you should know when choosing the time to take a trip to Maui:

Peak Season (December to March):

This season overlaps with winter in the continental United States, making it a popular time for vacationers looking to escape colder regions. Expect increased travel and lodging costs, as well as heavier crowds at popular attractions. The weather is generally good, with temperate temperatures and little rain.

Mid-Season (April to May and September to November):

These months provide a good balance between favorable weather and smaller crowds. Flights and hotels are typically less expensive, and you will have more flexibility in booking activities.

Off-Peak Season (June to August):

While summer is considered the off-peak season, it is also the time when families travel due to school vacations. Expect warmer temperatures and more humidity. Prices are typically lower than in peak season, although some attractions may still be crowded.

Booking Flights To Maui

Maui's primary airport is Kahului Airport (OGG), which is located on the island's northern shore. Kahului Airport, a significant transport hub, offers multiple daily flights for domestic and international destinations. Here's what you should know when booking flights to Maui:

Domestic Flights:

Major airlines like Hawaiian Airlines, Alaska Airlines, American Airlines, Delta Air Lines, and

United Airlines offer direct flights to Maui from various mainland cities, including Los Angeles, San Francisco, Seattle, and Denver. Nonstop flights are the most convenient alternative, however connecting flights are also available, frequently via Honolulu (HNL).

International Flights:

Maui is accessible from several international locations, with flights from Canada, Japan, and other Pacific Rim countries. Most international flights connect via Honolulu, so you may need to plan an inter-island trip to go to Maui.

Booking Tips:

To secure the best deals on flights, consider booking several months in advance, especially if you're traveling during peak season. Use fare comparison tools and price alerts to monitor ticket price movements.

Arrival at Kahului Airport

Upon your arrival at Kahului Airport, you will discover a well-equipped facility designed to accommodate both domestic and international tourists. The airport provides a wide range of services, including vehicle rental firms, shuttle services, and taxi stands. Here's a closer look at what to expect upon arrival:

Customs and Immigration: International travelers will clear customs and immigration at their first point of entry into the United States, usually Honolulu, before traveling to Maui. .Domestic travelers will proceed directly to baggage claim upon arrival at Kahului Airport.

Baggage Claim: The airport has a conventional baggage claim area with several carousels to accommodate arriving flights. Travelers should refer to the monitors for information on their flight's allocated carousel.

Ground Transportation: Kahului Airport has a variety of ground transportation choices, including rental automobiles, shuttle services, taxis, and public transport. Many hotels and resorts offer complimentary shuttle services for their visitors.

Navigating Transportation in Maui

Once you arrive in Maui, you'll need to decide which form of transportation is best for exploring the island's attractions. Maui has a number of options to meet varied interests and budgets, including rental automobiles and public transportation. Here's a closer look at the available means of transportation in Maui:

Rental Cars:

Renting a car is one of the most popular methods to see Maui, as it allows travelers more flexibility and convenience. A rental car allows you to explore rural regions, picturesque drives, and popular sights at your own time. Here's everything you should know about renting a car in Maui:

Rental Agencies: Kahului Airport is home to numerous major vehicle rental businesses, including Hertz, Avis, and Alamo. To ensure availability and the lowest pricing, book your rental car ahead of time, particularly during peak season.

Driving Tips: Driving in Maui is generally simple, with well-maintained roads and adequate signage. However, be prepared for tiny, curving roads, especially on routes such as the Hana Highway. Familiarize yourself with local traffic rules and always drive safely.

Parking: While most attractions and hotels have parking lots, some popular places may have limited parking options. Consider coming early to obtain a spot, and always follow stated parking rules to avoid fines.

Public Transportation:

For budget-conscious travelers or those who prefer not to drive, Maui's public transportation system provides an affordable alternative for getting around the island. Here's a closer look at this facet:

The Maui Bus: Operated by the County of Maui, the Maui Bus system connects significant sites such as Kahului, Lahaina, Kihei, and Wailea. The bus system provides both fixed-route and commuter services, with prices typically ranging between $2 and $5 each ride. While the bus is a cost-effective choice, keep in mind that service is limited in more rural places.

Schedules and Routes: The Maui Bus follows a set schedule, with route and timetable information available online or at major bus stops. Plan your trips ahead of time, and allow for extra travel time during peak hours or busy seasons.

Taxis and Ride-Share Services:

Taxis and ride-sharing services, such as Uber and Lyft, are extensively available in Maui and provide convenient transportation for guests who do not have rental automobiles.

Taxi Services: Taxis can be found at Kahului Airport, major hotels, and famous tourist destinations. While taxis are a dependable alternative for short excursions, the charges might be somewhat pricey for longer distances. It is best to confirm rates with the driver before starting your journey.

Ride-Sharing Services: Uber and Lyft are popular alternatives to traditional taxis, with competitive rates and the simplicity of app booking. Ride-sharing services are extremely handy for those who do not want to drive or use public transportation.

Biking and Walking:

Maui's compact size and diversified scenery make it an attractive destination for cyclists and walkers. While not a significant form of transportation, cycling and walking provide unique opportunities to appreciate the island's natural splendor.

Biking: Maui has various bike-friendly areas and designated trails, offering possibilities for both leisurely and demanding rides. Popular riding destinations include the Haleakalā downhill ride, West Maui loop, and beach pathways in Kihei and Lahaina. Several companies offer rentals and guided trips to suit different varieties of skill levels and interests.

Walking: Many of Maui's towns and attractions are pedestrian-friendly, making it an enjoyable way to discover local shops, restaurants, and cultural institutions. Coastal boardwalks and nature pathways offer chances for scenic walks and hiking activities.

Inter-Island Travel

For travelers looking to explore beyond Maui, inter-island travel offers the opportunity to experience the diverse landscapes and cultures of Hawaii's other islands. Here's all you need know about traveling between the islands:

Flights:

Inter-island flights are the most convenient and efficient way to travel between the Hawaiian islands. Several airlines operate frequent flights from Kahului Airport to other islands, such as Oahu, the Big Island, and Kauai. In booking an Inter-island flight in Maui, here's all you need to know:

Hawaiian Airlines: As Hawaii's major carrier, Hawaiian Airlines operates many daily flights between Maui and other islands. The airline is renowned for its dependable service and low rates.

Southwest Airlines: Southwest Airlines has expanded its service to include inter-island flights, giving passengers more alternatives and lower fares.

Booking Tips: When booking inter-island flights, schedule them early in the day to allow for probable delays and optimize your time on the next island. Booking in advance can help you get better rates, especially during high travel months.

Ferries:

While less prevalent, ferry services provide an alternative mode of inter-island travel, offering a scenic and leisurely approach to access nearby islands. Here's all you need to know about ferries in Maui:

Maui-Lanai Ferry: The Expeditions ferry service connects Lahaina, Maui to Manele Bay, Lanai. The ferry has many daily departures and runs around 45 minutes each way. This option is suitable for day trips or short stays in Lanai.

Getting to Maui is the first step towards a wonderful trip to paradise. With careful planning and consideration of your travel preferences, you can guarantee a smooth and comfortable trip to the island. Whether you tour Maui by vehicle, bus, bike, or foot, the island's diverse landscapes and inviting spirit ensure an unforgettable vacation experience. As you plan your journey, embrace the spirit of aloha and prepare to be amazed by the beauty and wonders of this magnificent island.

CHAPTER THREE

Accommodation

Finding the ideal place to stay can set the tone for your entire trip to Maui. Maui has a wide choice of hotels to suit every taste and budget, including luxurious resorts with world-class amenities, charming inns that reflect the island's character, and budget-friendly options that do not sacrifice comfort. In this chapter, we will take a look at the various types of accommodations available, offer insider recommendations for selecting the ideal location, and highlight some of the top alternatives in each category.

Luxury Resorts and Spas

Maui's luxury resorts provide first-rate services, ensuring an exceptional visit. These resorts, which are largely found in the famous districts of Wailea, Kaanapali, and Kapalua, are well-known for their breathtaking ocean views, comprehensive amenities, and superb dining experiences.

Luxury Resorts and Spas in Maui

Maui is known for its magnificent resorts and spas, which provide opulent accommodations, world-class amenities and great services to discerning travelers. Here are five of the island's most popular and high-quality luxury lodgings, together with details on their features and rates:

Four Seasons Resort Maui at Wailea

Why stay here?

Located on the stunning Wailea beach in Maui, this renowned resort features spacious ocean-view rooms and suites, three saltwater pools, and access to Wailea beach. Travelers can enjoy great cuisine at three restaurants, including the award-winning Spago. The resort boasts a world-class spa that provides Hawaiian-inspired treatments and wellness programs. Snorkeling, scuba diving, and golfing on adjacent courses are popular recreational activities.

Price Range: The average price range is around $1,100 per night, with seasonal variations.

Grand Wailea, A Waldorf Astoria Resort

Why stay here?

Located on the beautiful Wailea beach in Maui, this resort boasts a gorgeous beachfront position and large grounds. It features nine pools, including a water park with slides and a lazy river. The resort has several dining options, including the renowned and popular Humuhumunukunukuapua'a restaurant. The Spa Grande, one of Hawaii's largest spas, offers a variety of treatments and hydrotherapy options. The resort also offers cultural programs and art tours.

Price Range: The average price range is around $800 per night, depending on season.

Andaz Maui at Wailea Resort

Why stay here?

Located on the stunning Mokapu Beach in Wailea, Maui, this eco-friendly resort offers a modern design with open-air spaces, and luxurious rooms with private lanais. Guests can enjoy four infinity pools, direct beach access, and distinctive dining experiences at restaurants such as Ka'ana Kitchen. The Awili Spa and Salon provides personalized treatments with local products. The resort offers activities including outrigger canoeing and lei-making lessons.

Price Range: The average price range is around $950 per night.

The Ritz-Carlton, Kapalua

Why stay here?

Located on the scenic Northwest coast of Maui, in a secluded area in Kapalua, this resort features beautiful rooms and suites with ocean views. It has six restaurants, including The Banyan Tree, which focuses on locally produced ingredients. The Ritz-Carlton Spa provides treatments inspired by ancient Hawaiian traditions. Travelers can enjoy two championship golf courses, tennis courts, and nature trails.

Price Range: The average price range is around $900 per night, varying with the season.

Montage Kapalua Bay

Why stay here?

Located on the beautiful shores of West Maui, nestled in Kapalua Bay, this exquisite resort offers residential-style accommodations, including one to four-bedroom villas with complete kitchens and spacious lanais. The resort features a tiered pool, a beachfront position, and the renowned Cane & Canoe restaurant. The Spa Montage provides a variety of treatments and health activities. Activities include paddleboarding, snorkeling, and cultural tours.

Price Range: The average price range is around $2000 per night.

Mid-Range Hotels and Inns in Maui

Maui's midrange hotels provide comfort, convenience, and affordability without sacrificing quality. Here are five popular and excellent mid-range options:

Maui Coast Hotel

Why stay here?

Located in Kihei, just steps from the pristine Kamaole Beach Park 1, this hotel offers modern rooms with private balconies and kitchenettes. Amenities include a swimming pool, hot tubs, and an on-site restaurant called Ami Ami Bar & Grill.

Guests can also use the complimentary bike rentals and fitness center.

Price range: The average price range is around $300 per night.

Napili Kai Beach Resort

Why stay here?

This resort, located on Napili Bay, offers spacious rooms and suites with kitchenettes and private lanai. Guests can enjoy four swimming pools, beachside access, and dinner at the Sea House Restaurant. The resort also offers snorkeling, golf, and cultural programs.

Price Range: The average price range is around $350 per night.

Hana-Maui Resort

Why stay here?

Nestled along the picturesque Hana Highway on Maui's eastern coast, this resort provides tranquil suites with garden or ocean views. The resort has two pools, a health center, and the Hana Ranch Restaurant. Guests can participate in activities like horseback riding and guided cultural tours.

Price Range: The average price range is around $500 per night.

Royal Lahaina Resort and Bungalows

Why stay here?

This resort, located on Kaanapali Beach, offers a variety of accommodations, including rooms, suites, and beach huts. There are three swimming pools, tennis courts, a coastal restaurant, and a traditional Hawaiian luau.

Price Range: The average price range is around $300 per night.

Maui Seaside Hotel

Why stay here?

This hotel in Kahului provides comfortable lodgings, with easy access to the airport and other nearby attractions. The hotel has an outdoor pool, an on-site restaurant, Tante's Island Cuisine, and reasonable price rates for guests.

Price Range: The average price range is around $200 per night.

These mid-range options strike a balance between comfort and cost, making them ideal for guests wishing to enjoy Maui's beauty and culture without breaking the bank.

Budget-Friendly Hostels and Rentals in Maui

For budget-conscious travelers, Maui offers a range of hostels and vacation rentals that provide affordable and comfortable lodging options. Here are five popular and excellent budget-friendly options:

Aloha Surf Hostel

Why stay here?

Located in Paia on Maui's scenic northshore, this hostel offers both dormitory and private rooms in a peaceful setting. Guests have access to a communal room and kitchen, as well as complimentary breakfast and Wi-Fi. The hostel offers free daily excursions of the island's highlights.

Price Range: Dorm beds go for about $50 per night, while private rooms cost around $120 per night.

Banana Bungalow, Maui Hostel

Why stay here?

This dynamic hostel located in Wailuku, near the stunning Iao valley, offers dormitories and individual rooms in a lively atmosphere. A hot tub, Wi-Fi, and free breakfast are among the amenities. The hostel also offers free tours and activities, such as snorkeling and hiking expeditions.

Price Range: Dorm beds go for about $45 per night, while private rooms cost around $110.

Tiki Beach Hostel

Why stay here?

Located on Front Street in Lahaina, Maui, this hostel offers dormitory and private rooms with a laid-back atmosphere. Guests can take advantage of a shared kitchen, a barbecue area, and access to surrounding beaches. The hostel rents equipment for activities like surfing and snorkeling.

Price Range: Dorm beds go for about $35 per night, while private rooms cost around $90 per night.

Days' Inn by Wyndham Maui Oceanfront

Why stay here?

Located on the stunning shores of Keawakapu Beach in Kihei, this oceanfront hotel offers basic oceanfront rooms with direct beach access, as well as an on-site fitness facility and café. It's ideal for budget-conscious guests looking for seaside accommodations.

Price Range: The average price range is around $250 per night.

Napili Sunset BeachFront Resort

Why stay here?

Napili Sunset BeachFront Resort, located on Maui's stunning Napili Bay, offers guests direct access to a pristine sandy beach and breathtaking ocean views. The resort features spacious condos with private lanais, fully equipped kitchens, and free Wi-Fi. Amenities include an outdoor pool, barbecue areas, and complimentary beach gear.

Price Range: The average price range is around $250 to $300 per night.

These accommodations cater to a wide range of demands and budgets, ensuring that every visitor can find the ideal location to stay while experiencing the breathtaking island of Maui. Maui has something for everyone, from luxury resorts that promise enjoyment to budget-friendly hostels that inspire adventure, ensuring that your Hawaiian holiday is unique.

Distinctive Accommodation; Cottages and Eco-Lodges

For a truly unique experience, consider staying in one of Maui's unique accommodations, such as cottages or eco-lodges. These alternatives provide a close connection to the island's natural beauty and culture. Here's a closer look at this aspect:

Heavenly Hana Paradise

Why stay here?

Nestled in Hana's lush sceneries, these secluded cottages provide a peaceful retreat from the hustle and bustle, while still being close to the island's attractions.

The Kulani Maui

Why stay here?

This eco-friendly retreat in Lahaina features treehouse-style villas nestled among lush gardens. It's a unique alternative for individuals looking to connect with nature.

Booking Tips and Safety Advice

When planning your Maui accommodation, keep the following guidelines in mind to ensure a smooth and pleasurable stay:

- **Book Early:**

    Popular accommodations tend to fill up quickly, especially during peak seasons. Make your arrangements well in advance, to obtain the greatest rates and availability.

- **Consider Location:**

    Select a place based on your interests and itinerary. West Maui is ideal for luxury and beach access, whilst Upcountry boasts a cooler climate and natural beauty.

- **Check Reviews:**

    Read recent guest reviews to ensure that the resort matches your expectations for cleanliness, service, and amenities.

- **Verify Amenities:**

  Confirm that the accommodation provides the services you require, such as Wi-Fi, parking, and air conditioning, particularly in remote places.

- **Stay Safe:**

  Be mindful of potential threats such as water currents and weather. Always follow local safety guidelines and suggestions.

Choosing the appropriate accommodations is an important component of your Maui vacation. Maui's accommodations cater to all travelers, whether they choose the opulence of a world-class resort, the charm of a mid-range inn, or the simplicity of a budget-friendly hostel. By taking into account your tastes, budget, and itinerary, you can locate the ideal place to unwind and recharge after a day of experiencing the island's breathtaking surroundings and lively culture. Enjoy your stay, and allow Maui's wonderful hospitality to make your vacation really unforgettable.

CHAPTER FOUR

Attractions and Activities

Maui is a paradise with diverse landscapes and distinct cultures. It is a place where lush rainforests, clean beaches, and volcanic landscapes meet to form a breathtaking backdrop for a variety of activities and attractions. Whether you are an adventure seeker, a history buff, or someone looking to unwind in a tropical setting, Maui offers a wide array of experiences. This chapter will walk you through the island's best attractions and activities, making your visit as enriching and pleasurable as possible.

Must-See Natural Attractions

Haleakalā National Park

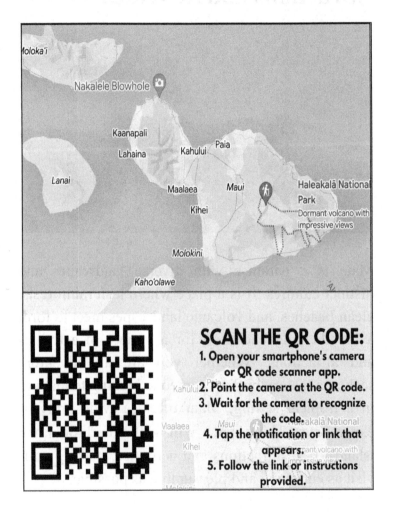

Located on the island of Maui, Haleakalā National Park is a must-see location for anybody visiting Maui. The park is home to the dormant Haleakalā Volcano, which is nearly 10,000 feet above sea level. Visitors frequently come to the peak to observe the beautiful dawn, which colors the sky in vivid shades of orange and pink.

Activities: Hiking trails abound in the park, ranging from simple walks to strenuous backcountry hikes. The Sliding Sands Trail provides a unique experience by allowing hikers to descend into the volcanic crater and explore its harsh, lunar-like terrain.

Tip: Sunrise viewing requires reservations, so prepare ahead. Dress warmly because temperatures at the peak can be quite low, even during the day.

Website: https://www.nps.gov/hale/index.htm.

The Road to Hana

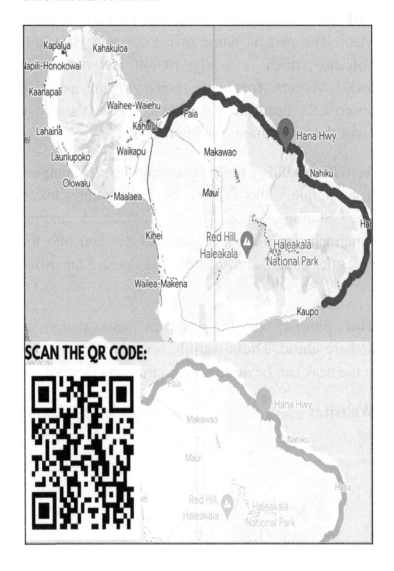

SCAN THE QR CODE:

Located on the northeastern coast of the island of Maui, The Road to Hana is one of Maui's most well-known attractions, providing a picturesque journey along the island's northeast coast. The journey is just as much about the destination as it is about the breathtaking scenery along the way.

Highlights: Along this meandering road, you'll see verdant jungles, tumbling waterfalls, and stunning ocean views. Notable destinations include the Twin Falls, Wai'anapanapa State Park with its black sand beach, and the peaceful village of Hana.

Activities: Explore the different hiking paths, swim in freshwater pools, and visit the historic Hana Town.

Tips: Leave early to avoid traffic and allow plenty of time to see the stops along the way. Drive carefully because the road is narrow and twisty.

Website: roadtohana.com.

Iao Valley State Monument

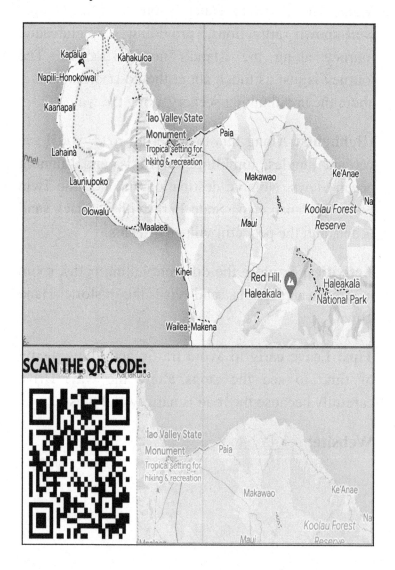

Located on the central part of the island of Maui, near Wailuku, Iao Valley State monument is a lush, verdant place famous for its breathtaking natural beauty and cultural significance. The monument's main attraction is the famed Iao Needle, a towering rock formation.

Activities: Take a leisurely walk along the trails, which provide stunning views of the valley and opportunity to learn about the area's rich history. The park is a fantastic location for photography and picnics.

Tips: The site might be crowded, so go early in the morning or late in the afternoon for a more relaxing experience.

Website: https://dlnr.hawaii.gov/dsp/parks/maui/iao-valley-state-monument/.

Beaches and Water Activities

Kaanapali Beach

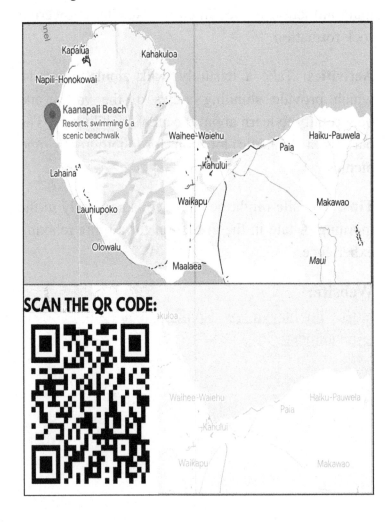

Located on the western coast of the island of Maui, near the town of Lahaina, Kaanapali Beach is one of Maui's most well-known beaches, with golden sands and blue waves. It's an ideal location for both relaxation and water sports.

Activities: Popular activities include snorkeling, swimming, and paddleboarding. The beach also hosts daily cliff diving ceremonies at Black Rock, which is a local tradition.

Tips: Arrive early to get a nice spot on the beach, and bring your snorkeling gear to explore the colorful underwater world.

Website: kaanapaliresort.com.

Wailea Beach

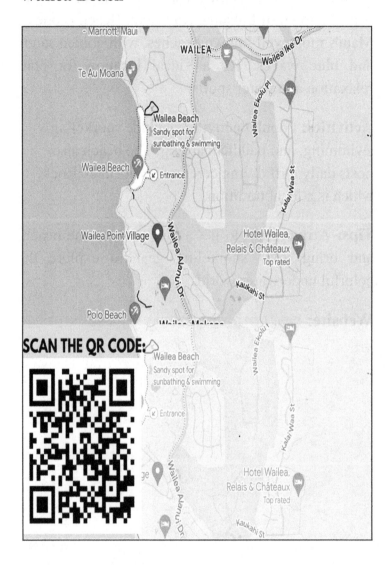

Located on the southwestern coast of the island of Maui, Wailea Beach, located in the upmarket Wailea resort area, has clean sand and quiet waters, making it excellent for sunbathing and swimming.

Activities: Activities include snorkeling and kayaking in the beautiful waters, or simply relaxing and admiring the breathtaking vistas of the neighboring islands.

Tips: The beach is easily accessible from adjacent resorts and has services including showers and restrooms.

Website: https://www.wailearesortassociation.com/beaches/wailea-beach.

Honolua Bay

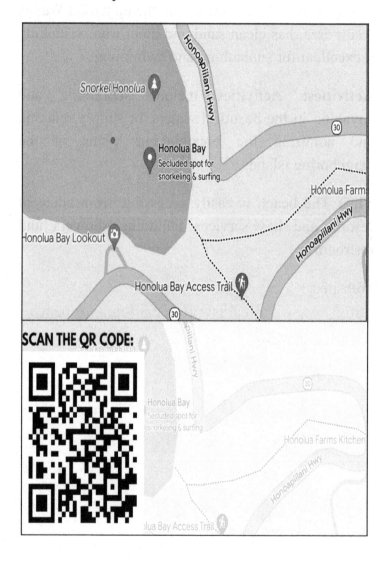

Located on the northwestern coast of the island of Maui, a few miles north of Kapalua, Honolua bay is a marine sanctuary known for its excellent snorkeling and diving opportunities. The area is rich with vivid coral reefs and a diverse marine life.

Activities: Snorkeling and scuba diving are the primary attractions here. The bay is also a famous surfing destination, particularly during the winter months.

Tips: Visit in the morning when the water is calm and visibility is optimal. Remember to respect the aquatic environment by not touching the coral.

Website: https://www.gohawaii.com/islands/maui/regions/west-maui/honolua-bay.

Cultural and Historical Sites

Lahaina Historic Town:

Located on the western coast of the island of Maui, along the shores of West Maui, Lahaina Historic Town, once the capital of the Hawaiian Kingdom, was a cultural hub rich in history and heritage and a thriving whaling village. In August 2023, a devastating wildfire engulfed the town, destroying significant landmarks and displacing residents. The community is now focused on rebuilding, preserving its cultural heritage, and supporting displaced residents

Attractions: Visit the Lahaina Historic Trail, which includes landmarks like the Baldwin Home Museum and the Lahaina Courthouse. The village also has art galleries, boutiques, and restaurants.

Activities: Immerse yourself in Hawaiian culture by attending a traditional luau, such as the Old Lahaina Luau.

Tips: Visit in the evening to enjoy the town's dynamic nightlife and stunning sunsets.

Website: lahainatown.com.

Maui Art and Cultural Center

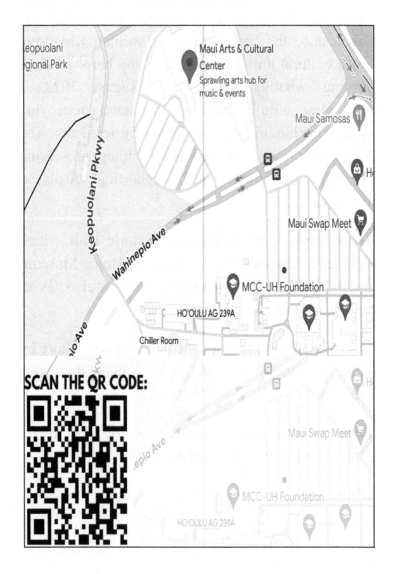

Located on One Cameron Way, near the intersection of Kahului Beach Road and Ka'ahumanu Avenue, the Maui Arts & Cultural Center (MACC) is the

island's principal cultural event and performance facility.

Activities: Enjoy concerts, theatrical plays, and art exhibitions featuring both local and international talent. The facility holds quite a number of events throughout the year, including the Maui Film Festival.

Tips: Plan your visit around an interesting performance or exhibition by checking the MACC's event calendar ahead of time.

Website: https://www.mauiarts.org.

Bailey House Museum:

SCAN THE QR CODE:

The Bailey House Museum, operated by Maui Historical Society is located at 2375 Main street, Wailuku and contains a wealth of Hawaiian history and antiquities. The museum, located in a 19th-century missionary residence, provides insights into Maui's history.

Attractions: The museum exhibits Hawaiian culture, early missionary life, and the island's natural history. The beautiful gardens that surround the museum are definitely worth exploring.

Tips: Guided tours are offered and provide useful context for the displays.

Website: https://mauimuseum.org.

Adventure Activities

Ziplining

Ziplining is a thrilling way to see Maui's natural beauty. Several businesses provide zipline tours through the island's gorgeous scenery.

Locations: Popular ziplining locations include the slopes of Haleakalā and the treetops of the West Maui Mountains.

Tips: Reserve your tour in advance, especially during peak tourist seasons. To maximize your experience, dress comfortably and wear closed-toe shoes.

Whale Watching

Maui is one of the best sites in the world to see whales, especially in the winter when humpback whales migrate to the warm Hawaiian seas to breed and give birth.

Tours: Whale watching tours depart from Lahaina Harbor and Maalaea Harbor, providing near interactions with these amazing creatures.

Tips: The ideal season for whale watching is from December to April. Bring binoculars and a camera to document the experience.

Surfing and Windsurfing

Maui's steady waves and trade winds make it ideal for surfing and windsurfing lovers.

Locations: Ho'okipa Beach is well-known for its windsurfing conditions, while novices can take lessons at Kaanapali or Kihei beaches.

Tips: If you are new to the activity, consider taking a session, since local instructors can provide helpful advice and maintain a safe environment.

Family-Friendly Activities

Maui Ocean Center

SCAN THE QR CODE:

Located at 192 Ma'alaea Road, on the island of Maui, the Maui Ocean Center is a popular family attraction that provides an interesting look at Hawaii's aquatic life.

Exhibits: The center's exhibits include interactive displays, a shark tank, and the world's largest collection of live Pacific corals.

Tips: Allow at least a couple of hours to completely tour the center, and consider engaging in one of the educational sessions available.

Website: https://molokinicrater.com/

Maui Tropical Plantation:

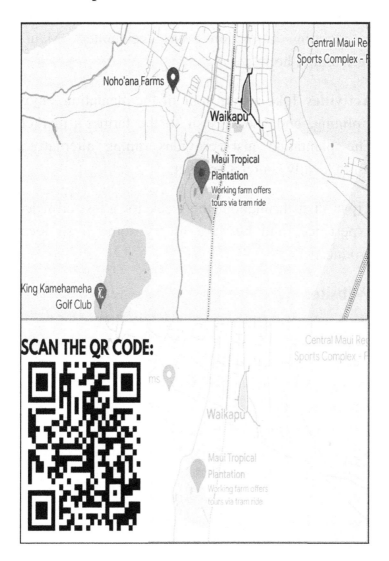

Located at 1670 Honoapi'ilani Highway, Waikapu, the Maui Tropical Plantation is an informative and entertaining attraction that celebrates Maui's agricultural heritage.

Activities Take a tram tour of the plantation, enjoy ziplining, and take a visit to the farmer's market. The plantation also provides dining alternatives using locally sourced products.

Tips: Visit throughout the week for a less crowded experience, and be sure to try some fresh local products.

Website:
https://www.mauitropicalplantation.com

CHAPTER FIVE

Food and Dining

Maui is a culinary paradise where unique flavors, fresh ingredients, and rich cultural traditions combine to create a thriving food scene. From indigenous Hawaiian food to international cuisines, Maui has a diverse culinary scene to suit all tastes and budgets. In this chapter, we will take a look at the island's culinary scene, showcasing its signature dishes, popular dining venues, and local food culture to ensure you enjoy a delicious tour through Maui's cuisine.

The Flavors of Maui

Maui's food reflects its diverse background, drawing from Polynesian, Asian, European, and American culinary traditions. The island's fertile soil and abundant ocean create a bountiful supply of fresh produce, seafood, and tropical fruits, which serve as the foundation for its culinary offerings.

Local Ingredients:

Maui's cuisine is distinguished by the use of fresh, locally sourced foods that accentuate the island's natural wealth.

Key Ingredients include:

- **Seafood:** The neighboring Pacific Ocean offers a variety of fresh seafood, including mahi-mahi, ahi tuna, opakapaka (pink snapper), and ono (wahoo). Seafood meals are frequently prepared simply to highlight the natural flavors.

- **Tropical Fruits:** Maui's tropical climate is suitable for growing pineapple, mango, papaya, and guava. These fruits are used in a variety of recipes, including fresh salads and desserts.

- **Produce:** Locally cultivated vegetables such as taro, sweet potatoes, and greens like kale and watercress are common ingredients in many Hawaiian cuisines. The island's farms also produce coffee, lavender, and macadamia nuts.

- **Beef and Pork:** Maui's ranches provide high-quality cattle, while traditional Hawaiian recipes frequently use pork, such as the famous kalua pig roasted in an underground oven.

Traditional Hawaiian Dishes

When visiting Maui, indulging in traditional Hawaiian cuisine is a necessity. These delicacies represent the island's history and cultural variety:

Poke

A traditional Hawaiian dish made with raw fish, usually ahi tuna, marinated in soy sauce, sesame oil, and green onions. Poke bowls are frequently topped with seaweed, avocado, and sesame seeds.

Loco Moco

A hearty cuisine that consists of rice topped with a hamburger patty, fried egg, and brown gravy. It is a popular comfort food among the natives.

Kalua Pig

This dish is traditionally slow-roasted in an imu (subterranean oven) until tender and smokey. It is frequently served at luaus and family gatherings.

Poi

Made from pounded taro root, Poi is a staple of Hawaiian cuisine. It has a distinctive, slightly sour flavor and is frequently served as a side dish.

Spam Musubi

A popular snack consisting of a slice of grilled Spam on top of rice and wrapped in seaweed. It reflects Hawaii's affinity for Spam, which is a World War II relic.

Exploring Maui's Culinary Scene

Maui is known not only for its beautiful beaches and verdant surroundings, but also for its thriving culinary scene. The island has a wide variety of dining options, from high-end luxury businesses to informal cafes and budget-friendly locales that cater to all tastes. This section provides a guide to some of Maui's most popular restaurants in various price ranges, highlighting their unique features, cuisines, and price range.

Luxurious Restaurants in Maui

Maui's opulent dining establishments provide exquisite cuisine and exceptional service, frequently coupled with beautiful vistas and sophisticated surroundings. Here are three luxurious dining options:

Mama's Fish House

Why dine here?

Mama's Fish House, located on the stunning beachfront in Paia, is well-known for its fresh fish and Polynesian-inspired cuisine. The restaurant's interior is decorated with Polynesian antiques, providing a warm and friendly atmosphere.

Cuisine:

Mama's Fish House specializes in seafood, including delicacies such as macadamia nut-crusted mahi-mahi, opakapaka in banana leaves, and ahi poke. The dessert buffet includes tropical goodies such as lilikoi (passion fruit) cheesecake and coconut haupia.

Price Range: Entrées range from $70 to $100, with the majority of meals costing around $100 per person, which includes appetizers and dessert.

Merriman's Maui

Why dine here?

Merriman's, located in Kapalua, has a spectacular seaside setting with views of the surrounding islands. The restaurant emphasizes farm-to-table eating, with 90% of its products obtained from Maui's farmers, fisherman, and ranchers. The ambiance is sophisticated but easygoing, with outdoor seating accessible to watch Maui's sunsets.

Cuisine:

The menu includes Hawaiian Regional Cuisine delicacies such as macadamia nut-crusted lamb, Kona lobster, and ahi poke with avocado. Merriman's also serves a popular brunch, including specialties like crab cake eggs benedict.

Price Range: Meal prices range from $20 and $50, with most dinners costing around $50 per person.

Lahaina Grill

Why dine here?

Lahaina Grill, located in the heart of Lahaina, has been a Maui dining institution for more than two decades. The restaurant is well-known for its innovative New American cuisine, which combines old techniques with new ingredients. The interior is attractively furnished, resulting in a classy dining ambiance.

Cuisine:

The menu features meals such as Kona coffee-roasted rack of lamb, seared ahi with vanilla bean jasmine rice, and seafood risotto. Lahaina Grill is well known for its triple berry pie and Road to Hana dessert.

Price Range: Entrée prices range from $40 to $65, with the majority of meals costing around $100 per person, including appetizers and dessert.

Mid-Range Restaurants in Maui

Maui's mid-range restaurants have good quality and diversified menus, offering great value for money while keeping high standards. Here are three popular and excellent mid-range dining options:

Hali'imaile's General Store

Why dine here?

Located in the pineapple plantations of Upcountry Maui, Hali'imaile General Store provides a unique dining experience in a plantation-style building. The restaurant is well-known for its unique menu, which represents the diverse culinary influences of Hawaii.

Cuisine:

Popular dishes include Sashimi Napoleon, which combines fresh fish and crunchy wontons, baby back ribs with Asian slaw, and the well-known pineapple upside-down cake. The menu also includes vegetarian options and locally sourced products.

Price Range: Entrée ranges from $30 to $50, with the majority of dinners costing around $50 per person, including drinks and dessert.

Star Noodle

Why dine here?

Located in Lahaina, Star Noodle is a famous place noted for its modern Asian food. The restaurant has communal seating and a casual, contemporary setting. It's popular with both locals and visitors due to its creative menu and robust flavors.

Cuisine:

The menu has a range of noodle meals, including garlic noodles, ramen, and pad Thai. Other popular dishes include pork buns, tempura shrimp, and miso salmon. Star Noodle also serves a variety of sake and craft cocktails.

Price Range: Entrée prices range from $15 to $25, with most meals costing around $40 per person, including drinks and desserts.

Café O'Lei

Why dine here?

This restaurant has outlets in Kihei, Lahaina, and Wailuku, and is recognized for its extensive food and courteous service. The restaurant provides a pleasant dining atmosphere with an emphasis on fresh, locally sourced ingredients. Café O'Lei is an excellent option for families and groups.

Cuisine:

The menu offers a variety of Hawaiian, American, and Asian-inspired meals, including macadamia nut-crusted chicken, seared ahi salad, and prime beef. The restaurant also serves a popular sushi menu and daily specials.

Price Range: Entrée prices range from $20 to $35, with the majority of meals costing around $40 per person, including drinks and dessert.

Budget-Friendly Restaurants in Maui

For those looking to enjoy tasty meals without breaking the bank, Maui has various budget-friendly options that do not compromise flavor or quality. Here are three popular and excellent budget-friendly dining options:

Paia Fish Market

Why dine here?

Originally established in Paia, this casual eatery has expanded to Lahaina and Kihei. Paia Fish Market is recognized for its ample amounts and fresh fish served in a relaxed setting. The communal seating creates a welcoming and social dining environment.

Cuisine:

The menu includes fish tacos, seafood pasta, grilled fish burgers, and platters featuring mahi-mahi and ono. The restaurant also serves vegetarian meals and homemade desserts.

Price Range: Entrée prices range from $12 to $20, with the majority of meals costing around $20 per person.

Da Kitchen

Why dine here?

With locations in Kahului and Kihei, Da Kitchen is well-known for serving hearty portions of traditional Hawaiian and local favorites. The relaxed and warm setting makes it ideal for a quick and tasty dinner.

Cuisine:

The cuisine features loco moco, kalua pork, chicken katsu, and the renowned Spam musubi. Da Kitchen is also noted for its plate lunches, which include a big serving of protein, rice, and macaroni salad.

Price Range: Entrée prices range from $10 to $15, with the majority of meals costing around $15 per person.

Tin Roof

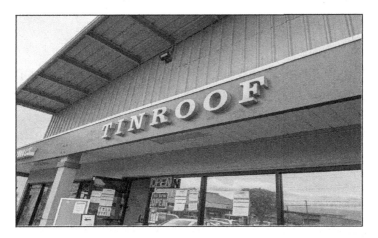

Why dine here?

Tin Roof, owned by "Top Chef" finalist, Chef Sheldon Simeon, is a tiny counter-service eatery in Kahului that serves comfort food with a local touch.

The restaurant is famous among both locals and visitors due to its tasty food and reasonable costs.

Cuisine:

The menu includes delicacies such as garlic shrimp, mochiko chicken, and poke bowls, all served over rice with a variety of toppings. Tin Roof also serves daily specials and unusual inventions such as "Kau Kau Tins," which mix many flavors in a single dish.

Price Range: Entrée prices range from $10 to $15, with the majority of meals costing around $15 per person.

CHAPTER SIX

Shopping

Shopping in Maui is more than just a pastime; it allows you to immerse yourself in the island's rich culture and bring a piece of paradise home with you. From busy local markets and artisan shops to luxury boutiques and souvenir stores, Maui has a wide range of shopping options to suit all tastes and budgets. In this section, we will walk you through Maui's top shopping destinations, highlight distinctive local products, and offer recommendations for making the most of your shopping experience.

Local Markets and Souvenirs

Local markets in Maui have a diverse range of handmade goods, fresh fruit, and one-of-a-kind souvenirs. These marketplaces offer an insight into the island's culture and people, featuring everything from home-made crafts to tropical fruits. Here are examples of some popular local markets in Maui:

Maui Swap Meet

Maui Swap Meet is a lively open-air market held every Saturday morning at the University of Hawaii Maui College in Kahului. Vendors sell a wide range of things, including locally made crafts, jewelry, apparel, and fresh vegetables.

- **Highlights:** Visitors can find unique items such as; hand-carved wooden bowls, Hawaiian textiles, and locally created artworks. The market is also an excellent opportunity to try local foods and tropical fruits such as papayas and pineapples.

- **Tips:** Arrive early to beat the crowds and get the best deals. Some sellers may not accept credit cards, so bring cash.

Upcountry Farmers' Market

This farmers market in Upcountry, Puhlani, Maui, takes place on Saturday mornings and sells organic fruit, locally-made cuisine, and handmade crafts.

- **Highlights:** The market is well-known for its locally grown fruits and vegetables, which include unique products such as dragon fruit and purple sweet potatoes. Customers can also find homemade jams, baked foods, and natural skincare products.

- **Tips:** Take time to chat with merchants, who are typically eager to share their knowledge about their items and the island.

Artisan Shops and Crafts

Maui's artisan shops are ideal for people looking for unique, handcrafted items that represent the island's cultural heritage and artistic flare. These shops frequently display items by local artists and crafters. Here are examples of some popular artisan shops and crafts in Maui:

Makawao

Makawao, located in the center of Upcountry Maui, is noted for its dynamic arts scene and beautiful boutiques. It is an excellent choice for anyone seeking to discover Maui's artistic side.

- **Highlights**: Visitors can explore galleries and stores that sell artisan jewelry, pottery, paintings, and sculptures. Hot Island Glass is a famous place to see glass blowing demonstrations and buy beautiful glass artwork.

- **Tips:** Schedule your visit around the town's weekly First Friday event, which includes live music, art exhibitions, and special promotions.

Hana Coast Gallery

The Hana Coast Gallery, located at the Travaasa Hana Resort, features excellent art and crafts by over 200 Hawaiian artisans. The gallery showcases a carefully curated selection of paintings, woodwork, and textiles.

- **Highlights:** The gallery is famous for its collection of Hawaiian quilts and koa wood furniture. It's an excellent site to find high-quality, one-of-a-kind items.

- **Tips:** Take your time exploring the gallery's wide selections and consider scheduling a personalized tour.

Fashion and Boutiques

Maui's fashion scene combines tropical charm and modern trends, with a variety of businesses catering to both locals and visitors. Maui's boutiques cater to all tastes, from beachwear to high-end couture. Here are examples of some popular fashion boutiques in Maui:

The Shops at Wailea

This upscale shopping center features a mix of luxury goods, local boutiques, and excellent dining options. The Shops at Wailea provide a quality shopping experience in an idyllic location.

- **Highlights:** Shoppers can explore stores like Louis Vuitton, Tiffany & Co., and Tommy Bahama, as well as local favorites Mahina and Sand People, which offer trendy island-inspired clothing and accessories.

- **Tips:** Check the calendar for upcoming events and live performances at the center, which will enhance your shopping experience.

Front Street

Lahaina's Front Street is a busy hub for shopping, dining, and entertainment. The street is lined with a variety of establishments, including art galleries and souvenir stores.

- **Highlights:** Popular shops include Lahaina Printsellers for vintage maps and artwork, Maui Hands for local art, and Maui Clothing Company for casual and resort attire.

- **Tips:** Visit in the evening for a leisurely stroll while admiring the bustling atmosphere and ocean vistas.

Specialty Stores and Unique Finds

There are several specialty stores in Maui that provide one-of-a-kind products and experiences. These establishments are ideal for acquiring presents or mementos that embody the spirit of Maui. Here are examples of some specialty stores and unique finds in Maui:

Maui Tropical Plantation

Maui Tropical Plantation, located near Waikapu, serves as both a tourist attraction and a shopping location for a range of local products. The plantation houses the Country Store, which sells souvenirs, tropical-themed goods, and local cuisine.

- **Highlights:** Shoppers can find Maui-grown coffee, macadamia nuts, and handcrafted soaps. The plantation also provides tours that teach visitors about Hawaii's agricultural legacy.

- **Tips:** Don't miss the tasting room, where you can try locally manufactured wines and spirits.

Ali'i Kula Lavender Farm

Ali'i Kula Lavender Farm, located in the hills of Upcountry Maui, provides a unique shopping experience focused on lavender-based items. The property offers breathtaking views of the island and a tranquil ambiance.

- **Highlights**: The farm shop offers a diverse selection of products, including lavender-scented lotions, soaps, and culinary items such as lavender honey and tea.

- **Tips:** Take a guided tour to learn about the various types of lavender grown on the farm and enjoy a complimentary cup of lavender tea.

Shopping Tips and Etiquette

When shopping in Maui, keep these tips in mind to improve your experience and help the local community:

- **Shop Local:** Buying locally created products helps Maui's economy and craftspeople. Look for things that say "Made in Hawaii" or "Made in Maui."

- **Bargaining:** While haggling is customary in some markets, keep in mind that many vendors set reasonable prices for their handmade goods. When bargaining, always show respect and politeness.

- **Sustainable Practices:** Consider bringing reusable shopping bags to help reduce plastic waste and be conscious of the environmental impact of your purchases.

- **Cultural Sensitivity:** Respect the cultural value of specific artifacts, such as Hawaiian textiles or koa wood goods, and learn about their history and meaning.

Shopping in Maui is a delightful exploration of the island's culture and ingenuity. Maui's shopping venues cater to every interest and budget, from small markets full of homemade treasures to exquisite stores featuring the latest designs.

CHAPTER SEVEN

Customs and Etiquette

Understanding and respecting local customs and etiquette is crucial for any traveler, as it enhances the experience and promotes pleasant relationships with the local population. Cultural traditions of Maui, like the rest of Hawaii, are strongly founded in tradition and respect for the land and people. This chapter will walk you through the most significant customs and etiquette in Maui, assisting you in navigating social situations while also showing respect for the island's culture and population.

The Spirit of Aloha

At the center of Hawaiian culture is the concept of "aloha", a term that means more than just a hello or goodbye. Aloha represents love, compassion, kindness, and a sense of mutual respect. It is a way of life that values harmony and connectedness to others and the natural environment. The following are the core components of this facet:

- **Embrace Aloha:**

  Visitors are encouraged to demonstrate the spirit of aloha by being kind, friendly, and respectful to everyone they meet. When interacting with locals or other travelers, a pleasant smile and genuine appreciation can go a long way.

- **Cultural Sensitivity:**

  To demonstrate cultural sensitivity, learn a few simple Hawaiian terms and phrases, such as "mahalo" (thank you) and "e komo mai" (welcome). This shows respect for the local culture and improves your communication.

Greeting and Communication

Hawaiians have their own manner of greeting and communicating, which frequently incorporates traditional practices with modern norms. The following are the core components of this facet:

- **Hawaiian Greeting:**

  The "honi" is a traditional Hawaiian greeting in which people touch their noses and foreheads while exchanging breaths. While this is less popular in current times, it is nevertheless used in some cultural contexts. A handshake or pleasant hug is more common in everyday contact.

- **Use of Hawaiian Language:**

  While English is commonly spoken, incorporating Hawaiian words to your vocabulary demonstrates respect and interest in the local culture. Common expressions include "aloha" (hello/goodbye/love), "mahalo" (thank you), and "ohana" (family).

- **Communication Style:**

  Hawaiians frequently use a calm and laid-back communication style. Maintain patience and openness while avoiding aggressive or confrontational conduct. When conversing with locals, take the time to listen and express genuine interest in their stories and experiences.

Respect For Nature and Sacred Sites

Maui's natural beauty is vital to its culture and identity. Respect for the land, or "aina," is a core component of Hawaiian values. The following are the core components of this facet:

- **Leave No Trace:**

  When visiting Maui's natural attractions, such as beaches, parks, and hiking trails, remember to "leave no trace." Dispose of waste appropriately, follow indicated pathways, and avoid disturbing wildlife.

- **Sacred Sites**:

  Maui has many sacred sites, including Haleakalā, Iao Valley, and temples. Respect the sacred structures by following the given signs and rules and refraining from climbing or touching them. When visiting these sites, visitors are encouraged to be quiet and reflective.

- **Cultural Practices:**

  Take part in traditional traditions such as "malama aina," which signifies caring for the earth. This can include activities like beach cleanups and conservation campaigns.

Dress Code and Attire

Maui's warm environment and beach lifestyle influence its dress code, which is often casual and laid back. However, there are some conventions to consider:

- **Beach Attire:**
  Swimwear is appropriate at the beach or pool, however it is customary to cover up with a

shirt or wrap when leaving these areas. Walking around in your swimsuit away from the beach is considered impolite.

- **Casual Dress:**

  Casual, comfy clothes are appropriate for most events. For dining out or attending events, resort wear or smart casual attire is often appreciated.

- **Formal Occasions:**

  Wear modest clothing at formal events or religious sites. Men may wear pants and a collared shirt, while women could opt for a dress or blouse with a skirt.

Social Etiquette and Interaction

When interacting with Maui locals, it's critical to be aware of societal conventions and expectations. The following are the core components of Maui's social etiquette and interactions:

- **Personal Space:**

  Hawaiians cherish personal space and may like to maintain some distance during interactions. If you've just met someone, don't stand too near or touch them until they invite you to.

- **Photographs:**

  Always seek permission before taking photos of people, particularly at cultural events or when visiting local communities. This demonstrates respect for their privacy and culture.

- **Gifts and Offerings:**

  If you are invited to someone's home, consider bringing a little gift, such as a dessert or a local product. It's an expression of thanks and respect for their hospitality.

Celebrating Hawaiian Culture

Participating in Maui's cultural customs and festivals is an excellent way to demonstrate respect and admiration for the local heritage. The following are the core components of Maui's customs and culture:

- **Cultural Events:**

  Attend cultural festivals and events, such as the Aloha Festivals or the Maui Film Festival, to learn about Hawaiian traditions, music, and dance. Participate respectfully and learn from the natives.

- **Hula and Music**:

  Enjoying hula performances and listening to Hawaiian music is an important element of the Maui experience. Show your appreciation by applauding performers and participating in the cultural narratives shared through these arts.

General Travel Etiquette

Being a polite and respectful traveler leads to a pleasant experience for both you and the local community. The following are the core components of Maui's general travel etiquette:

- **Punctuality:**

    Despite the casual pace of life in Maui, punctuality is still valued, particularly for tours and events.

- **Local Businesses:**

    Support local businesses and craftsmen by purchasing their goods and services. This not only benefits the local economy, but it also allows you to bring home unique keepsakes.

- **Respect for Diversity:**

    Maui's population is diversified, with a variety of ethnic backgrounds. Show respect for diverse customs and traditions by remaining open-minded and nonjudgmental.

CHAPTER EIGHT

Itineraries and Suggestions

Planning a trip to Maui entails more than just choosing your flights and lodgings. The island has a wide range of activities and attractions to suit every type of traveler, from adventurers to those looking for relaxation. This chapter includes extensive schedules and tips to help you make the most of your vacation, whether you have just a few days or a couple of weeks on the island. Each schedule is designed to highlight Maui's natural beauty, cultural heritage, and lively food scene, resulting in an amazing experience.

Weekend Getaway: A Three-Day Itinerary

Day One: Arrival and Relaxation:

- **Morning**: Arrive at Kahului Airport to pick up your rental car. Go to your hotel to check in and relax.

- **Afternoon:** Begin your Maui vacation with a relaxing afternoon at Kaanapali beach. Enjoy swimming, sunbathing, and snorkeling.

- **Evening:** Depending on your budget, head to Lahaina for supper at either Lahaina Grill or Paia Fish Market. After that, visit Lahaina's historic town and bustling Front Street.

Day Two: Road to Hana:

- **Early Morning:** Depart early for the Road to Hana. Pack snacks and drinks, as the drive could last all day.

- **Stops Along The Way:** Make a visit to Twin Falls, Wai'anapanapa State Park's black sand beach, and the tranquil village of Hana.

- **Afternoon:** Head to Ohe'o Gulch (Seven Sacred Pools) for a lovely trek and swim.

- **Evening:** Return to your hotel and enjoy supper at Café O'Lei in Kihei.

Day Three: Haleakalā Sunrise and Upcountry Exploration:

- **Early Morning:** Get up early to watch the dawn at Haleakalā National Park. Dress warmly because it can get cold at the summit.

- **Morning:** Descend the mountain and enjoy breakfast at Kula Lodge in Upcountry Maui.

- **Afternoon:** Visit the lovely towns of Makawao and Paia, which are famous for their art galleries, boutiques, and local restaurants.

- **Evening:** Depending on your schedule, head to the airport or have a final dinner at Mama's Fish House.

One-Week Adventure: A Seven-Day Itinerary

Day One: Arrival and Beach Day:

- **Morning:** Arrive at Maui, pick up your rental car, and check into your lodging.

- **Afternoon**: Spend the day at Wailea Beach, enjoying the beautiful dunes and quiet waves.

- **Evening:** Dine at the posh restaurant; Ferraro's Bar e Ristorante, located in Wailea.

Day Two: Snorkeling at Molokini Crater:

- **Morning:** Schedule a snorkeling tour to Molokini Crater, a half submerged volcanic caldera famous for its dynamic marine life.

- **Afternoon:** Return to the mainland and rest at your hotel or visit neighboring Kihei.

- **Evening:** Have dinner at Kihei's renowned Three's Bar & Grill, which serves Hawaiian, Southwestern, and Pacific Rim food.

Day Three: Lahaina and Kaanapali:

- **Morning:** Explore the old village of Lahaina, including the art galleries and the Lahaina old Trail.

- **Afternoon:** Visit Kaanapali Beach for swimming and sunbathing. Take part in a traditional Hawaiian cliff diving ceremony at Black Rock.

- **Evening:** Enjoy a sunset at Old Lahaina Luau, with authentic Hawaiian cuisine and performances.

Day Four: Road to Hana:

- **Full Day:** Spend the full day touring the Road to Hana, visiting important places such as Wai'anapanapa State Park and Wailua Falls.

- **Evening:** Return to your accommodation for a restful evening.

Day Five: Upcountry Maui:

- **Morning:** Drive to Upcountry Maui to visit the Ali'i Kula Lavender Farm and Surfing Goat Dairy.

- **Afternoon:** Visit the Maui Wine vineyards and tasting room in Ulupalakua.

- **Evening:** Dine at Kula Bistro, known for its wonderful Italian and American cuisine.

Day Six: Haleakalā National Park and Makawao:

- **Early Morning:** Experience the sunrise at Haleakalā National Park, followed by a trek along the Sliding Sands Trail.

- **Afternoon:** Explore the lovely village of Makawao, with its stores and art galleries.

- **Evening:** Dine at Hali'imaile General Store, which serves unique island cuisine.

Day Seven: Departure:

- **Morning:** Spend your last morning in Maui relaxing at the hotel or touring neighboring beaches.

- **Afternoon:** Return your rental car and depart from Kahului Airport, reminiscing on a week of memorable memories.

Themed Itineraries

Family Friendly Adventure:

- **Day 1:** Explore the Maui Ocean Center and play at Kalama Beach Park.

- **Day 2:** Explore Haleakalā National Park and enjoy a family lunch in Upcountry Maui.

- **Day 3:** Immerse yourself in culture by attending a family-friendly luau, such as the Feast at Lele

.

Romantic Escape

- **Day 1:** Enjoy a couple's massage at a spa in Wailea, followed by a romantic dinner at Ko Restaurant.

- **Day 2:** Enjoy a scenic helicopter flight and a sunset dinner cruise.

- **Day 3:** Explore isolated beaches like Secret Beach in Makena and stargaze at Haleakalā.

Ecotourism and Nature

- **Day 1:** Visit the Maui Nui Botanical Gardens and hike the Waihee Ridge trail.

- **Day 2:** Volunteer at the Maui Ocean Center or a local environmental initiative.

- **Day 3:** Visit the Kealia Pond National Wildlife Refuge and the Maui Forest Bird Recovery Project.

Day Trip Ideas

- **Lanai Adventure:** Take a ferry from Lahaina to Lanai for a day of exploring, visiting Hulopoe Bay and the Garden of the Gods.

- **Molokai Exploration:** Fly to Molokai and spend the day exploring Kalaupapa National Historical Park and the Halawa Valley.

- **Whale viewing:** During whale season (December to April), take a whale watching tour from Lahaina Harbor.

Final Tips and Suggestions

- **Plan Ahead:** Reservations are recommended for popular activities, especially during peak seasons. Consider arranging tours and dining experiences ahead of time to reserve your spot.

- **Balance Your Itinerary:** To ensure a well-rounded experience, alternate between active and relaxing days. Maui's pace is relaxed, so take time to appreciate the island's natural beauty.

- **Explore Local Culture:** Connect with Maui's rich cultural legacy by attending local events, visiting museums, and taking part in cultural activities.

- **Maintain Flexibility:** Weather conditions and personal tastes can change, so be open to adjusting your itinerary as needed.

Maui's diverse scenery, rich culture, and wide range of activities provide limitless options for discovery and adventure. Whether you're on a short vacation or a longer visit, these itineraries and tips will help you make the most of your time on this magical island, creating memories that will last a lifetime.

CHAPTER NINE

Local Events and Festivals

Maui is a thriving island where culture, history, and community combine to produce a calendar packed with fascinating local events and festivals. These events provide a look into the island's unique cultural fabric, bringing islanders and visitors together to enjoy music, dancing, food, and customs that embody the spirit of aloha. This chapter covers some of Maui's most popular events and festivals, emphasizing the island's distinct blend of Hawaiian heritage and modern influences.

Annual Events and Festivals

Maui Film Festival

The Maui Film Festival, held in June in Wailea, is a much anticipated event. The festival, known for its open-air screenings under the stars, offers a broad range of independent films, documentaries, and short films from around the world. Attendees can enjoy screenings at a variety of locations, including the Celestial Cinema at the Wailea Golf Course, where films are projected onto a massive outdoor screen.

- **Highlights:** In addition to film screenings, the festival organizes a number of special activities, such as filmmaker forums, award ceremonies, and celebrity parties. The Taste of Wailea event provides a gastronomic experience featuring meals from Maui's premier chefs.

- **Tips:** Buy tickets ahead of time for popular movies and events, and bring a blanket or a low-back chair for outdoor films.

Maui County Fair

The Maui County Fair is an annual event held in Wailuku each fall, usually in October. As one of Maui's greatest community events, the fair draws thousands of people with its carnival rides, games, food booths, and live entertainment.

- **Highlights:** The fair includes a procession, a petting zoo, and various competitions such as floral arrangement and home economics. Malasadas and shave ice, as well as teriyaki plates and poke bowls, are among the delicious treats available from local food sellers.

- **Tips:** To avoid crowds, go on weekday evenings or early in the morning, and check the schedule for live performances and special events.

East Maui Taro Festival

The East Maui Taro Festival, held in April in the town of Hana, honors the importance of taro in Hawaiian culture. The celebration encourages the preservation and growth of taro, a staple food in traditional Hawaiian cuisine.

- **Highlights:** The festival features hula performances, Hawaiian music, arts and crafts, and educational exhibits about taro growing and its cultural significance. Local vendors sell taro-based meals including poi and kulolo, a sweet taro dessert.

- **Tips:** Plan an overnight stay in Hana to thoroughly enjoy the festival and explore the surrounding area, including the picturesque Hana Highway and Haleakalā National Park.

Cultural Festivals

Makawao Rodeo

The Makawao Rodeo is a unique event that celebrates Maui's paniolo (Hawaiian cowboy) tradition. The rodeo, held annually over the Fourth of July weekend, is a highlight of Upcountry Maui's calendar, attracting participants and spectators from across the islands.

- **Highlights:** The rodeo includes traditional sports including bull riding, calf roping, and barrel racing. The festivities begin with a parade, which include floats, marching bands, and horses. Visitors can also enjoy live music, food booths, and craft vendors.

- **Tips:** Get there early to obtain a good viewing area, and bring sunscreen and a hat for sun protection.

Maui Arts and Cultural Center Events

The Maui Arts & Cultural Center (MACC) in Kahului holds a number of cultural events throughout the year, such as concerts, theatrical performances, and art exhibitions. The MACC is a focus for artistic expression and cultural exchange, drawing both local and international talent.

- **Highlights:** Popular events include the Hawaiian Slack Key Guitar Festival, Maui Classical Music Festival, and the Maui Ukulele Festival. The facility also offers dance performances, film screenings, and lectures.

- **Tips:** Plan your visit around an interesting performance or exhibition by checking the MACC's event calendar ahead of time.

Music and Dance Performances

Aloha Festivals

The Aloha Festivals are a statewide celebration of Hawaiian culture that take place every September. Maui holds a number of events as part of the festival, including hula performances, Hawaiian music concerts, and cultural displays.

- **Highlights:** The festivals seek to conserve and promote Hawaiian culture via traditional arts, crafts, and ceremonies. Events often include lei-making workshops, Hawaiian language classes, and storytelling sessions.

- **Tips:** Attend the workshops and activities to obtain a better grasp of Hawaiian culture and heritage.

Maui Jazz and Blues Festival

The Maui Jazz and Blues Festival is an annual event that brings together well-known musicians from Hawaii and beyond. The festival, which takes place at several places throughout the island, has a combination of jazz and blues concerts, workshops, and jam sessions.

- **Highlights:** The festival showcases both established and rising performers, providing a varied range of performances. The venues vary from intimate bars to outdoor stages with breathtaking ocean views.

- **Tip:** Buy tickets in advance for popular shows, and consider attending workshops to learn more about the genres and methods.

Local Celebrations

Lahaina Banyan Tree Birthday

The Lahaina Banyan Tree Birthday commemorates one of Maui's most recognizable monuments. The banyan tree at Lahaina's Courthouse Square was planted in 1873 and is Hawaii's largest, offering a spectacular canopy over the town's central gathering spot.

- **Highlights:** The event features live music, cultural events, and art installations. Local vendors sell crafts, jewelry, and food, creating a bustling atmosphere beneath the sprawling branches of the banyan tree.

- **Tips:** Visit the neighboring museums and historical places in Lahaina to discover more about the town's fascinating past.

BONUS SECTION

Maui, with its magnificent landscapes, rich cultural heritage, and dynamic society, provides a wealth of experiences beyond the usual tourist attractions. To properly appreciate the island, it is beneficial to know a few exclusive tips and recommendations to enhance your vacation. This section will give you helpful tips from residents and experienced tourists to help you make the most of your time in Maui:

Embrace the Aloha Spirit

One of the most important aspects of visiting Maui is embracing the "aloha spirit," which includes love, harmony, and mutual respect. Here's how to immerse yourself in this distinctive facet of Hawaiian culture:

- **Be Respectful:** Respect local customs and traditions. This involves being mindful of sacred sites, adhering to etiquette at cultural events, and treating locals and other travelers with compassion and consideration.

- **Participate in Cultural Activities:** To learn more about Hawaiian traditions and customs, try hula dancing, lei-making, or visiting a luau.

Discover Hidden Gems

While Maui's well-known attractions are absolutely worth visiting, the island also has quite a number of hidden gems that provide unique and memorable experiences:

- **Explore the Upcountry:** Head to Maui's Upcountry district for cooler temperatures and stunning vistas of the island. Visit local farms, art galleries, and botanical gardens in towns like Makawao and Kula.

- **Visit Local Beaches:** While Kaanapali and Wailea are popular, consider visiting lesser-known beaches like Hamoa Beach in Hana or Napili Bay, where you can enjoy a more calm ambiance and pristine sands.

- **Hike Off-the-Beaten-Path Trails:** Explore Maui's natural beauty by hiking off-the-beaten-path paths like the Waihee Ridge Trail or the Pipiwai Trail in Haleakalā National Park. These trails provide breathtaking views and lush scenery.

Make The Most of Your Time

Maximizing your time on the island will improve your overall experience. Here are some recommendations to help you prepare and enjoy your vacation more efficiently:

- **Plan for the Road to Hana:**

  This picturesque trip is a must-do, but it can take a full day to visit all of the highlights. Start early to avoid traffic and have plenty of time to explore. Consider spending the night in Hana to truly experience the area's splendor and serenity.

- **Book Activities in Advance:**

  Popular activities like snorkeling tours, helicopter flights, and sunrise visits to Haleakalā National Park tend to fill up quickly. To prevent disappointment, it is recommended that you reserve your spot before-hand.

- **Be Flexible with Your Itinerary:**

  Make time for spontaneity and leisure. While planning is vital, leaving room for unexpected adventures can result in some of your most memorable moments.

Dining and Shopping Tips

Maui's culinary culture and retail opportunities provide numerous opportunities to sample native flavors and products. Here are some dining and shopping recommendations for you to try:

- **Local Food Trucks:** Some of Maui's tastiest cuisine can be found at local food trucks. Geste Shrimp Truck in Kahului and Thai Mee Up near the airport are both great places to get tasty and economical meals.

- **Visit Farmers' Markets:** To support local farmers and craftsmen, visit markets like the Upcountry Farmers Market in Pukalani or the Maui Swap Meet in Kahului. You'll find fresh food, handcrafted items, and one-of-a-kind keepsakes.

- **Support Local Artisans:** When shopping for souvenirs, look for locally manufactured items like Hawaiian quilts, handcrafted jewelry, or koa wood sculptures. This not only benefits the local economy but also ensures that you bring home a piece of Maui's culture.

Basic Hawaiian Phrases and Vocabularies

Greetings and Basic Expressions:

- **Aloha** - Hello/Goodbye/Love.

- **Mahalo** - Thank you.

- **'A'ole pilikia** - You're welcome/No problem.

- **E kala mai** - Excuse me/Sorry.

- **Pehea 'oe?** - How are you?

- **Maika'i** - Good / Fine.

- **A'ole** - No.

- **'Ae** - Yes.

- **Pomaika'i** - Good luck.

- **A hui hou** - Until we meet again/Goodbye.

Common Questions:

- **He aha kēia?** - What's this?
- **Ehia kālā?** - How much is it?
- **I hea ka hale waihona puke?** - Where's the library?
- **I hea ke kahua mokulele?** - Where's the airport?
- **Aia i hea ka hale'aina?** - Where's the restaurant?
- **I hea ka hale, ho'okipa?** - Where's the hotel?
- **Aia i hea ka lua?** - Where is the restroom?
- **He aha, ka manawa?** - What time is it?
- **Pehea e hiki ai i laila?** - How do I get there?
- **He mea, 'ai kona?** - Do you have food?

Directions and Transportation:

- **Akau** - North.
- **Hema** - South.
- **Hikina** - East.

- **Komohana** - West.
- **Holo:** - Go/Travel.
- **Pa'a ka'a** - Stop.
- **E holo kākou!** - Let's go!
- **Ka'a 'ōhua** – Bus
- **Ka'a'ō** – Taxi
- **Ka'a'ō i nā'ono eha** - Four-wheel-drive car.

Shopping and Numbers:

- **Kāka'ikahi** - How much does it cost?
- **Mākaukau** - Read.
- **Kēia** - This.
- **Kēlā** - That.
- **Kālā** - Money.
- **Ewalu** - Eight.
- **'Elua** - Two.

Dining and Food:

- **Pā'ina** - Meal or party.
- **'Ono** - Delicious.

- **Mauʻu** - Vegetables.

Weather and Nature:

- **Ua** - Rain.
- **La** - Sun.
- **Makani** - Wind.
- **Kai** - Sea.
- **Pua** - Flower.
- **Lā** - Day.
- **Po** - Night
- **Mālie** - Calm.
- **Hu'ihu'i** - Cold
- **Wela** - Hot.

These basic Hawaiian phrases and vocabulary words can help you navigate Maui more easily and show respect for the local culture. Enjoy your trip on the island, and don't be afraid to use these phrases to interact with people and improve your experience!

Contact Information and Resources in Maui

When visiting Maui, having access to important contact information and resources can improve your travel experience and ensure a pleasant stay. Here are some key contacts and resources for visitors:

Emergency Services

- **Emergency Number:** Dial 911 for police, fire, or medical emergencies.

- **Maui Memorial Medical Center:** Located in Wailuku, this is the island's major hospital. Phone number: (808) 244-9056.

Visitor Information

- **Maui Visitors Bureau:** Provides information about attractions, events, and accommodations.

- **Website:** visitmaui.com

- **The Hawaii Tourism Authority:** Offers comprehensive travel information and resources for all Hawaiian islands.

- **Website:** gohawaii.com

Transportation

- **Maui Bus Public Transit System:** Offers island-wide service with routes connecting key towns and attractions.

- **Website:** mauicounty.gov/607/Maui-Bus.

- **Kahului Airport (OGG):** Maui's principal airport, offering flights from the mainland U.S. and inter-island connections.

- **Website:** airports.hawaii.gov/ogg.

General Information

- **Maui County Government:** Provides resources and information about public services and activities.

- **Website**: mauicounty.gov.

- **Local News:** 'Maui Now' provides up-to-date news and events.

- **Website:** mauinow.com.

Having this information at your fingertips guarantees that you have the necessary support and direction for a safe and pleasurable trip to Maui.

Safety Tips

Ensuring your safety and well-being is critical for a stress-free holiday. Here are some tips to ensuring your safety and well-being:

- **Stay Hydrated:** Maui's tropical environment can be dehydrating, particularly during outdoor activities. Drink plenty of water and take regular rests to avoid heat exhaustion.

- **Be Cautious in the Ocean:** Ocean conditions can change quickly. Pay heed to warning signs and advisories at beaches, and never turn your back on the waves. If you aren't a good swimmer, consider wearing a life jacket.

- **Drive carefully:** Maui's roads, particularly the Road to Hana, are small and winding. Drive carefully, follow the speed limit, and be aware of other drivers and pedestrians.

Exploring Maui with these exclusive tips and advice will improve your trip and allow you to experience the island like a local. Embrace the aloha attitude, search out hidden jewels, and immerse yourself in Maui's rich culture and natural beauty, which combine to make it a truly unique destination. Following these tips will not only make your trip unforgettable, but will also help to preserve and appreciate this spectacular island paradise. Enjoy your tour around Maui, and may your experiences leave you with long-lasting memories and a stronger connection to the island and its people

Made in the USA
Coppell, TX
17 November 2024

40416462R00095